Native Pollinators

Butterflies

Roberta Baxter

PUBLISHERS

2001 SW 31st Avenue
Hallandale, FL 33009
www.mitchelllane.com

First Edition, 2020.

Author: Roberta Baxter
Designer: Ed Morgan
Editor: Sharon F. Doorasamy

Names/credits:
Title: Butterflies / by Roberta Baxter
Description: Hallandale, FL :
Mitchell Lane Publishers, [2020]

Series: Native Pollinators

Library bound ISBN: 9781680203783

eBook ISBN: 9781680203790

Library of Congress Cataloging-in-Publication Data
Names: Baxter, Roberta, 1952- author.
Title: Butterflies : native pollinators / by Roberta Baxter.
Description: First edition. | Hallandale, FL : [2020] | Series: Native pollinators | Includes bibliographical references and index.
Identifiers: LCCN 2018030949| ISBN 9781680203783
 (library bound) | ISBN 9781680203790 (ebook)
Subjects: LCSH: Butterflie—Ecology—Juvenile literature.
 | Insect pollinators—Juvenile literature. | Pollination by insects—Juvenile literature.
Classification: LCC QL562.6 .B38 2020 |
 DDC 595.78/9—dc23
LC record available at https://lccn.loc.gov/2018030949

Photo credits: freepik.com, Shutterstock.com, Vecteezy.com

Contents

Butterflies are rock stars of the insect world. They are beautiful. They float on the air. Everyone loves to watch them.

Butterflies are **pollinators**. They **pollinate** flowers to make seeds. The seeds grow into plants.

Eastern tailed-blue

Pollinators spread **pollen** from flower to flower. Pollen is a powder found inside flowers. **Nectar** is inside flowers too. Butterflies love nectar. It is sweet.

American lady butterfly

Butterflies reach into flowers to drink nectar. Pollen sticks to their wings and legs.

The butterfly goes to another flower. Pollen comes off. The flower is pollinated. It can make seeds now.

West Coast lady

13

Some butterflies are **natives**. Natives have lived in America from the earliest times. There are several natives with the name Swallowtail. One is the Eastern Tiger Swallowtail. Another is the Western Tiger.

Western Tiger Swallowtail

15

Butterflies hatch out of eggs. A baby is called a caterpillar. It eats leaves and grows bigger. Then it makes a covering over itself. This is a **chrysalis**. After a while, it breaks out of the chrysalis. It is a butterfly.

Monarch butterfly

17

The Monarch butterfly is famous. Monarchs are known for flying 3,000 miles for the winter. This trip is known as their **migration**. Monarchs lay their eggs on plants called milkweed.

Monarch butterfly

Butterflies see red, green, and yellow. They like sweet smells. Butterflies help many flowers make seeds so more plants can grow.

Orange-barred sulfur

MAIN BODY PARTS OF A Butterfly

Butterflies have three main body parts. The head includes the eyes that can see all around. The wings and legs are attached to the **thorax**. The **abdomen** is the back part of the butterfly. Some butterflies have spots that look like eyes on their wings. This scares away anything that might eat the butterfly.

Scales cover the bodies of butterflies. It is easiest to see them on the wings. The brilliant colors of butterflies come from the scales. If you touch a butterfly, brown powder will show up on your fingers. It is scales from the wings. They are attached loosely and come off easily. Losing scales does not hurt the butterfly if it is only a few.

wings

abdomen

thorax

GLOSSARY

abdomen
The back part of a butterfly which has the heart and intestines

chrysalis
Hard covering where a caterpillar stays until it has turned into a butterfly

migration
A long flight that Monarch butterflies take to another place for the winter

native
A butterfly that has lived in America from the earliest times; not from another country

nectar
A sugary drink found inside flowers

pollen
A powder found inside flowers

pollinate
To take pollen from one flower and take it to another flower which allows that flower to turn into fruit

pollinators
Insects, birds, or animals that spread pollen from one flower to another

thorax
Middle part of a butterfly that holds the wings and the legs

23

FURTHER READING

Heiligman, Deborah. *From Caterpillar to Butterfly.* New York: HarperCollins, 2015.

Delano, Marfe Ferguson. *National Geographic Kids: Butterflies.* Washington, DC: National Geographic Children's Books, 2014.

Rattini, Kristin Baird. *National Geographic Readers: Seed to Plant.* Washington, DC: National Geographic Children's Books, 2014.

Pollination (Science Readers: Content and Literacy). Teacher Created Materials, 2014.

ON THE INTERNET

http://www.enchantedlearning.com/subjects/butterfly/allabout/
The site has lots of information about butterflies, their life cycle, and what they eat.

http://www.butterflywebsite.com/educate/birthofbutterfly.cfm
This site has a lesson plan for grades 1 and 2 about how butterflies are born.

https://www.kidsbutterfly.org/
There are a variety of resources on this page, including frequently asked questions, photographs and coloring pages about butterflies.

https://www.thebutterflysite.com/facts.shtml
Answers to many questions about butterflies, including a section on the Monarch butterfly, can be found at this site.

INDEX

ABOUT THE AUTHOR

Roberta Baxter enjoys writing about science and history. She likes to see the different species of butterflies that pass through Colorado every year and even has a butterfly bush in her yard to attract butterflies.